S0-BYB-928

>> CODE POWER: A TEEN PROGRAMMER'S GUIDE™

GETTING TO KNOW
HTML
Code

JEFF PRATT

rosen publishing's
rosen
central®

New York

Published in 2019 by The Rosen Publishing Group, Inc.
29 East 21st Street, New York, NY 10010

Copyright © 2019 by The Rosen Publishing Group, Inc.

First Edition

All rights reserved. No part of this book may be reproduced in any form without permission in writing from the publisher, except by a reviewer.

Library of Congress Cataloging-in-Publication Data

Names: Pratt, Jeff (Software developer), author.
Title: Getting to know HTML code / Jeff Pratt.
Description: First Edition. | New York : Rosen Publishing, 2019. | Series: Code Power : a teen programmer's guide | Includes bibliographical references and index. | Audience: Grades 5–8.
Identifiers: LCCN 2018008323| ISBN 9781508183693 (library bound) | ISBN 9781508183716 (pbk.)
Subjects: LCSH: HTML (Document markup language)—Juvenile literature.
Classification: LCC QA76.76.H94 P735 2019 | DDC 006.7/4—dc23
LC record available at https://lccn.loc.gov/2018008323

Manufactured in the United States of America

{ CONTENTS

$menuclass = 'horiznav';
$topmenuclass ='top menu

The computer age. The digital revolution. The information age. No matter what it is called, not since the Industrial Revolution—when industry and machine manufacturing replaced farming—has the entire world been changed so very much by technology. Computers and the internet have completely transformed the way people do almost everything: work, learn, shop, create, play, and even how people communicate.

No computer language has been more responsible for all this change than HTML. HTML (Hypertext Markup Language) is very easy to learn and also easy to deliver on laptops, phones, toys, e-readers, or anything else with a computer in it. Very quickly, HTML brought the internet from a few thousand computer hobbyists and academics in the 1980s to where it is today: more than one billion websites being used by three billion people— almost half the world—each day.

HOW DID IT HAPPEN SO FAST?

HTML was more accessible than any computer language before or since for the average person. First, web browsers (examples of web browsers include Microsoft Internet Explorer,

Apple Safari, Mozilla Firefox, and Google Chrome) were on every computer and could show the content created by HTML code in a way that looked good and was simple to use. As for programming in HTML, most people could launch their first website in a few days because HTML used straightforward terms someone with no programming background could understand.

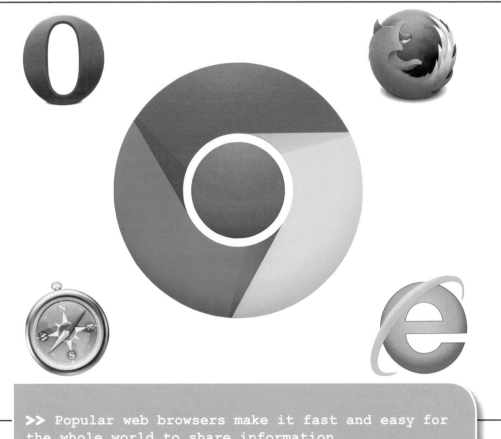

>> Popular web browsers make it fast and easy for the whole world to share information.

For instance: <Color=blue> and <bold>. This code tells the text to appear blue and bold—no programming jargon required.

With such a simple programming language behind it, the internet exploded in the 1990s, and millions of businesses and ordinary people discovered how to easily and quickly explore, collect, and share information online in a world now connected by computers. From entire libraries to collections of pictures, video, and music, people across the world could now display content and ideas for everyone else to find. Almost immediately, the internet (helped by HTML) provided shopping, live discussions, entertainment, polls, health services, online classes—just about everything people wanted.

>> HTML is the code behind many of the websites people use every day.

Of course, over time, HTML has changed. HTML5 is the fifth update of HTML used as the industry standard. The language is always adding new elements and tools to keep up with the demand of people online who want to do and see new things. Still, most of the code is the same as what was first written way back in 1990.

Today, it is a code used by professional computer programmers as well as small business owners, bloggers, and pet owners looking to share the best pictures of their cat.

While HTML is the primary force behind the internet and most websites, pages that are more interactive typically require programmers who know other languages to add to the HTML (such as CSS, JavaScript, Java, and PHP, among others). However, learning HTML is the perfect starting point. It can lead you to learning these other languages and more about software and web development as a profession. With more and more business being conducted online every day, the need for employees who know web development has never been greater.

CHAPTER 1

JOINING THE HTML REVOLUTION

T he age of computers began when they were integrated into businesses and homes throughout the 1970s and 1980s.

Computers were great. They stored information, enabled one to make business charts, did complicated math and accounting, and even had some fun games, too. Eventually, people started sharing information either directly, from computer to computer, or over the earliest form of what is now a global internet. At first, only some advanced computer scientists and hobbyists knew how to make their computers talk to other computers. There was not yet an easy way for the average person to share information.

>> Computers first became popular with businesses in the 1970s and then arrived in homes in the 1980s.

In 1989, an English physicist named Tim Berners-Lee wrote a memo proposing that his organization (CERN, the European Organization for Nuclear Research) design and use a simpler language for its hundreds of computer systems to share information across the internet. He called his language HTML, or Hypertext Markup Language. "Hypertext" indicated that the text would easily hyperlink (or link) to other pages. "Markup" means that someone could literally mark up the words with bold, italics, colors, underlines, or different fonts. In 1990, Berners-Lee wrote the first browser and server software to make this new simple language work. Berners-Lee argued that HTML would be perfect for encyclopedias, online help, documentation, tutorials,

>> Tim Berners-Lee, who first proposed and invented HTML code, is considered a founding father of the modern internet.

news, collaborative authoring (several authors working on the same project), and personal notebooks.

In 1991, CERN introduced HTML and the World Wide Web to the rest of the world. Decades later, there are more than a billion websites and half the world uses the internet every day. One of the reasons HTML has taken off so quickly is because of how easy it is to use, even for beginners.

>>A BRIEF HISTORY OF THE INTERNET (AND HTML)

- 1973: The University College of London (England) and the Royal Radar Establishment (Norway) connect via a system called ARPANET; the term "internet" is born.
- 1976: Queen Elizabeth II sends her first email.
- 1985: Symbolics.com, a computer company, launches the first website.
- 1990: Tim Berners-Lee, a physicist at CERN, develops HTML.
- 1992: The first audio and video files are distributed over the internet.
- 1993: There are now six hundred websites online. The White House maintains one of them.
- 1995: Microsoft releases its first web browser: Internet Explorer.
- 1995: Compuserve, America Online, and Prodigy begin to provide internet access to consumers. Amazon, Craigslist, eBay, and Match.com go live.
- 1998: Google launches.

- 2004: Facebook launches.
- 2005: YouTube and Reddit launch.
- 2006: Twitter launches.
- 2010: Pinterest and Instagram launch.
- 2013: More than half of all American adults now do their banking online.
- 2018: More than one billion websites are online.

>> The internet exploded in the 1990s, thanks largely to the release of Windows 95, which included the Internet Explorer browser.

There is a tradition among computer programmers of using the phrase "Hello, World!" as a test message when learning and testing a new language. This custom likely comes from a famous programmer book *The C Programming Language*, first published in 1978. The example program from that book prints "hello, world" (without capital letters or an exclamation point) and is believed to have been borrowed from a 1974 Bell Laboratories internal memo.

Creating an HTML page to display "Hello, World!" is pretty easy. To begin, open Notepad (on a PC) or TextEdit (on a Mac) on your computer. Then, all you have to do is write some HTML. For instance, just type "Hello, World!" While this may seem too easy, typing some text like that is part of HTML code. Now, save this file as helloworld.htm. The .htm at the end is the first clue for web browsers that they are looking at an HTML file and should display the code accordingly. You can create as many new .htm files as you want now. Or just keep working with the

>> First published in 1978, *The C Programming Language* book started the custom of learning new code with a "hello, world" program.

>>CRACK THE CODE

There are no secrets with HTML. Most web browsers provide an easy way to see all the HTML—the background code—of any web page. It is a great opportunity for new HTML programmers to learn code and get a peek at another programmer's work. It is also perfect when testing their own webpages to see how browsers are understanding their code. Pressing the Control and U keys at the same time opens up the source code for most browsers on a Windows computer. For Mac users, a website's code can be viewed by pressing the Command, Option, and U keys at the same time.

same helloworld.htm file—but remember to save after making changes.

Finally, you can view your HTML code in any web browser. There are two ways to do this. Either drag your helloworld.htm file into an open browser on your desktop, or right-click the file and select the browser you want to use to view the file. You should now be looking at your HTML page as displayed by a web browser. Your browser should display:

Hello, World!

This may not be the most exciting page on the internet, but—if it worked—it is a good start. This "markup language" was designed to do much more with text.

CHAPTER 2

SHOW SOME STYLE: PAGE DESIGN

H TML was first developed specifically to display text in a web browser. The "Markup Language" part of its name refers to the fact that the code tells the web browser how to display (or mark up) a web page's words.

```
36    a#logo_link2 {
37      display:none;
38    }
39
40
41    .screen0 a#logo_link2 {
42        width: 26%;
43        height: 200px;
44        display: block;
45        background-image: url("img/logo_big.png");
45        background-repeat: no-repeat;
546       background-size: contain;
547       position: absolute;
648       top: 10px;
649       ft: 36%;
65
```

>> Cascading Style Sheets describe and set the presentation of a document written in a language like HTML.

To tell browsers how to display text beyond the basic, HTML uses HTML tags and Cascading Style Sheets (CSS). These are some of the core components of the entire language.

HTML TAGS

HTML tags tell web browsers to display this tagged text in a very specific way. Tags can put text in bold, bulleted lists, new paragraphs, different colors, subscript, different sizes, or highlight, among other effects.

HTML tags are recognized and created with the less-than (<) character and end with the greater-than (>) character, and the information between those two symbols tells the browser how to format and display the text.

Most HTML tags come in two parts—an opening and a closing. For example, <P> is the opening tag and </P> is the closing tag for a paragraph. Notice the special backslash character (/) used for the end tag. That tells the browser that is the end of the tagged text, and it can now focus on other things. This is how they work:

In your helloworld.htm page, for example, the text looks plain. There is nothing special about it. If someone changed the code to read <strong>Hello, World!</strong>, the new display would look something like this: **Hello, World!**

What happened there? It is relatively easy to see—which is what makes HTML so powerful and easy to use. The <strong> tag told the browser to show any words within the tag in bold. Using <b> </b> also works, but the current standard is to use <strong> </strong>. After the web browser sees </strong> (the end tag) in HTML code, it will stop displaying any further text in bold in the browser. To get bold characters again, a programmer simply has to create a new <strong> </strong> tag for whatever text they need to stand out.

There are many different tags in HTML, all with a specific purpose. For example, <em>Hello, World!</em> is displayed as: *Hello, World!* The <em> tag tells the browser to show words in italics to emphasize (where the "em" comes from) the word. Using <i> </i> also works, but the current standard is to use <em> </em>.

It is also possible to combine some tags, using two, three, or more all together at once. For example, <strong> <em>Hello, World</em> </strong> uses two tags at the same time and becomes ***Hello, World!***

It is important to note how the code is written so that the <em> tag is closed before the <strong> tag is closed. HTML tags should be "nested" in a proper order, meaning that the tag opened most recently should be the next tag to close. Otherwise, the browser (and programmer) can get confused when tags are opened and closed in random order, and the page will not display properly.

One of the great things about HTML is the flexibility. The code <em> <strong>Hello, World</strong> </em> also displays ***Hello, World!*** It does not matter which tag comes first, as long as the tags are closed in the correct, nested order.

Nesting might seem easy at first, but HTML can be nested many times, and it can be hard to keep track. For example: <center><em> <strong>Hello, World</strong> </em></center> will display:

Hello, World!

Another example: <center><strong>Hello, <em>World</em></strong></center> will display:

Hello, *World!*

There are some important differences between these lines of code. In the second, the <em> tag was only on World!, so only that word was italicized. Both words were within the <strong> tag, so the bold remains for both. There are many, many ways to combine text tags in HTML, and they will all work perfectly—as long as the programmer remembers to nest them.

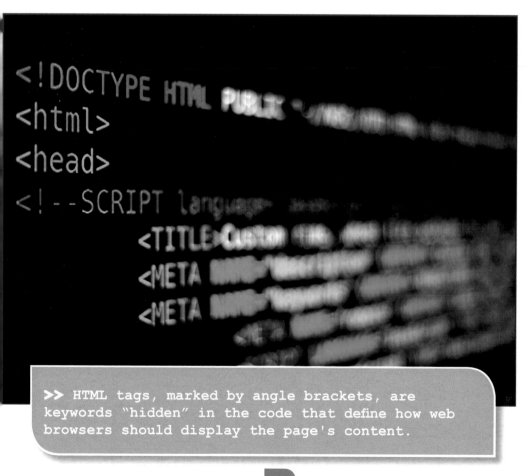

>> HTML tags, marked by angle brackets, are keywords "hidden" in the code that define how web browsers should display the page's content.

In addition to bold and italics, some important text tags are used to change the size, style, and color of the font used to display text. For example: <font size="3" face="arial" color="red">Hello, World!</font> will display:

Hello, World!

Users can experiment with the size, font type, and color of any text. It is also possible to use Cascading Style Sheets (CSS) to make these changes to text, but the method of using text tags is still recognized by all browsers—which are programmed to recognize code from 1990 if need be—and remains a great starting point for people new to HTML or programming.

>>WHO IS IN CHARGE?

The World Wide Web Consortium (W3C) is the primary international organization that oversees the internet's continued development, including ongoing updates to HTML. Web developers and companies that create browsers often disagree on the best way to use HTML or how to best integrate other languages into the web. It is up to the W3C to sort it all out, via an open forum for discussion, to help make sure everyone agrees on a standard that will keep web users happy. To do so, there have been six major editions of HTML. W3C was founded, and currently led, by none other than Tim Berners-Lee, the man who started it all.

Version	Year
HTML	1991
HTML 2.0	1995
HTML 3.2	1997
HTML 4.01	1999
XHTML	2000
HTML5	2014

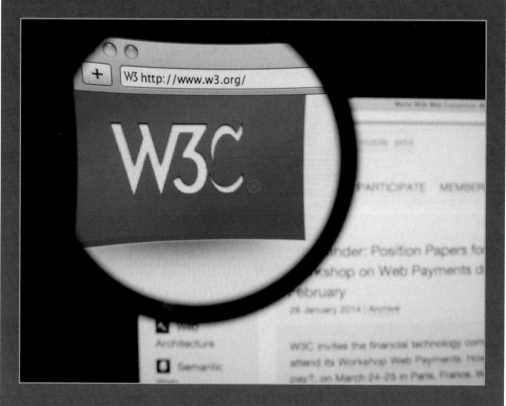

>> The World Wide Web Consortium (W3C) is the main international organization for the development of standards for the global internet.

The original goal of HTML was to better organize and present text, and it has some great ways to do that.

The tag <p> tells the browser to start a new paragraph. It will put some space between the last bit of text and the new.

<p>Here's some text to read.</p>
<p>And this is some more text.</p>

Like other text tags, the </p> closes the tag at the end of the paragraph. That lets the browser know that it is done with that specific paragraph.

The tag <br> inserts a single line break in the text.

Here's some text to read.
And this is some <br> more text.

Unlike other text tags, <br> is not used before and after the section of text a programmer wants to change. Rather, a single
 (there is no </br> tag) is placed where the coder wants to have a single line break inserted.

The tag <hr> inserts a horizontal line.

Here's some text to read.
And this is some more text.
<hr>

While not all websites need to make use of horizontal lines, they can be used to help make different sections of text more readable and pleasing to the eye.

>>COMBINING WITH HTML

Spark Creative Partners (based in Cincinnati, Ohio) is an advertising agency specializing in websites, social media, and marketing for famous authors, small businesses, nonprofit organizations, restaurants, and realtors. They have designed and managed thousands of websites. Spark's developers work in HTML, PHP, CSS, and JavaScript and also use a popular HTML-building software called WordPress for most of their clients. This software allows Spark to build websites quickly and for its clients to do some of the web work themselves without having to know how all that HTML code works. When needed, for something a little different or new, Spark's programmers will write special code for their clients. They make certain all of their sites are responsive—meaning they want to ensure the pages look good on any device on which they are viewed.

>> Wordpress, a popular free software that allows developers to easily create many special features for their websites, uses HTML.

MAKING A LIST

Another easy way to organize text is to use lists. HTML has two main types of lists: unordered and ordered. An unordered HTML list might look like this:

```
<h1>An Unordered HTML List</h1>
<ul>
  <li>Bigfoot</li>
  <li>Loch Ness Monster</li>
  <li>Chupacabra</li>
  <li>The Jersey Devil</li>
</ul>
```

This code would be interpreted by a web browser to look something like this:

An Unordered HTML List
- Bigfoot
- Loch Ness Monster
- Chupacabra
- The Jersey Devil

Little black bullets (discs) are the default when using the <li> </li> tag. To control the symbol used in unordered lists, users just add some code to the opening unordered list <ul> tag:
- <ul style="list-style-type:disc">
○ <ul style="list-style-type:circle">
■ <ul style="list-style-type:square">

An ordered HTML list might look like this:

```
<h1>An Ordered HTML List</h1>
<ol>
  <li>Bigfoot</li>
  <li>Loch Ness Monster</li>
  <li>Chupacabra</li>
  <li>The Jersey Devil</li>
</ol>
```

This code would display as:

An Ordered HTML List
1. Bigfoot
2. Loch Ness Monster
3. Chupacabra
4. The Jersey Devil

An ordered list is built on successive numbers (which is the default) instead of bullets. Just as with unordered lists, users can change this by adding a little more information (type="") to the opening ordered list <ol> tag.

<ol type="1"> lists items with numbers (this is the default 1, 2, 3, etc.)

<ol type="A"> lists items with uppercase letters (A, B, C, etc.)

<ol type="a"> lists items with lowercase letters (a, b, c, etc.)

<ol type="I"> lists items with uppercase roman numerals (I, II, III, etc.)

<ol type="i"> lists items with lowercase roman numerals (i, ii, iii, etc.)

Whether using unordered or ordered lists, to add more items to the list, a coder just needs to use another <li> tag—and must close it with an </li>.

Another way HTML organizes text is with description lists. A description list is a list of terms with a description of each term. The <dl> tag tells the browser it is a description list. The <dt> tag defines the term (name). The <dd> tag describes each term. For example:

```
<dl>
<dt>Nessie</dt>
<dd>- sea monster that lives in Loch Ness, Scotland</dd>
<dt>Morag</dt>
<dd>- sea monster that lives in Loch Morar, Scotland</dd>
 <dt>Champy</dt>
<dd>- giant lake monster living in Lake Champlain</dd>
</dl>
```

This code will display as:

Nessie
      - sea monster living in Loch Ness, Scotland
Morag
      - sea monster living in Loch Morar, Scotland
Champy
      - lake monster living in Lake Champlain

FORGET THE SPOONS—SET THIS TABLE

Another simple and effective way to present information is with a table. With tables, it is possible to deliver all sorts of information in neatly organized rows and columns. Textbooks, newspapers, and all other kinds of media use them all the time—and HTML makes it easy to make these for websites, too. With a quick look, visitors to a site or blog will find it very easy to read any data presented in a table.

To start off, a table needs a few tags to pull itself together. With just a few simple keystrokes, an HTML master can make all the tables they want, with dozens of columns, hundreds of rows, and thousands of pieces of data. Tables can include text, images, links to music, or just about anything the coder wants.

The tag <table style="width: 100%"> tells the browser to start a table and take up all ("100%") of the available window space. Then there is <tr> for a table row; <th> for a table header; and <td> for table data.

The first <tr> </tr> becomes the first row—or the header row. These <th> tags tell the browser what name to give the header of each column. There are three below, but if there were, for example 30 <th> tags, the table would have 30 columns.

The next <tr> </tr> entries become the info in the columns. The <td> tags tell the browser what info to put in the next row. There are three below, but, again, if there were 30 <th> tags, there would need to be 30 matching <td> tags. There should be a <td> tag for every <th> tag. For every new row, the code needs to be input all over again.

Once finished, tables can be concluded with a simple closed table tag: </table>. The browser will take care of the rest. The best way to see tables at work is to look at an example.

```
<table style="width: 100%">
<h2>HTML Table Example – Chupacabra Sightings!</h2>

<table style="width:100%">
 <tr>
    <th>Date</th>
    <th>Location</th>
    <th>Photo?</th>
  </tr>
  <tr>
    <td>12/26/1996</td>
    <td>Mason, Washington</td>
    <td>Yes!</td>
  </tr>
  <tr>
    <td>05/22/2001</td>
    <td>Eagle Pass, Texas</td>
    <td>No</td>
  </tr>
    <tr>
    <td>02/14/2018</td>
    <td> Thoreau, New Mexico</td>
    <td>Yes!</td>
  </tr>
 </table>
```

This example of code would become:

HTML Table Example – Chupacabra Sightings!

Date	Location	Photo?
12/26/1996	Mason, Washington	Yes!
05/22/2001	Eagle Pass, Texas	No
2/14/2018	Thoreau, New Mexico	Yes!

The possibilities with tables are endless. Coders can change the headings, add rows and columns, and do all kinds of other cool stuff. The browser will use the HTML defaults as far as color and text appearance are concerned, but these can all be easily changed later with some more code.

CHAPTER 3

MAKE THE CONNECTION: HYPERLINKS

The internet is built on hyperlinks—clickable words and pictures that lead to other pages. Even if a website only points to itself (which is very rare), if it has a menu and multiple pages, it uses links. An example of a hyperlink is a photo that a user can click on to go through a gallery of more photos. Or an ad or a funny cat video is a hyperlink since it takes the user to

>> Hyperlinks allow users to move around the internet easily via clickable words and pictures that lead to other pages.

a new page. When a user searches for something on the web, the search engine create a huge list of links to choose from. The ability of programmers to code hyperlinks is part of what makes the web work so well.

>>HOW THE INTERNET FINDS THINGS

The most popular search engines (sites that specialize in finding information and websites) all use special programs called web crawlers that continuously search the internet all day long, every day, constantly discovering new web pages and revisiting old ones to see if anything has changed. Every time a web crawler visits a page, it makes a copy of the page and then follows every link on that page and makes copies of those pages and so on, adding it all to a huge index from which it can search for "funny cat videos" later. Websites such as Google, Bing, Yahoo, Ask.com, and Baidu are all examples of search engines with web crawlers that find new hyperlinks every day.

>> HTML is an important piece of the code that runs the world's most popular search engines.

HTML links are built, just like text, by using various tags. Here is one example:

Visit <a href="http://www.lochnesssightings.com" target="_self">Loch Ness Monster Sightings!</a> for the latest Loch Ness monster sightings.

If this code is opened using any browser, it will appear as:

Visit <u>Loch Ness Monster Sightings!</u> for the latest Loch Ness Monster sightings.

Clicking this hyperlink (which is now underlined to show that it will take the user somewhere else) will lead a user straight to www.lochnesssightings.com.
Taking a closer look at that code will reveal what it is really doing.

<a href="**http://www.lochnesssightings.com**" target="_self">Loch Ness Monster Sightings!</a>

The opening <a> tag is called an anchor element (thus the <a>) and tells the browser that a link is coming.

<a href="http://www.lochnesssightings.com" target="_self">Loch Ness Monster Sightings!</a>

The href=" " within the <a> tag tells the browser what website, webpage, or link to go to. Every hyperlink tag must include this part, or the clickable text will not know where to go. It is important to notice that the link is between opening and closing quotations: " "

<a href="http://www.lochnesssightings.com" target="_self">Loch Ness Monster Sightings!</a>

The target=" " within the <a> tag tells the browser where the link should be opened. If the tag does not include this, the link defaults to the same browser window (which is also what "_self" would do). The other popular option is "_blank," which opens up the page in a whole new window or tab.

<a href="http://www.lochnesssightings.com" target="_self">Loch Ness Monster Sightings!</a>

All words before the tag closes, with the </a>, will appear online as the hyperlink. The entire phrase or title becomes clickable.
<a href="http://www.lochnesssightings.com" target="_self">Loch Ness Monster Sightings!</a>

Finally, the hyperlink tag is closed by using an </a> to let the browser know the hyperlink is over.

Using this general format, HTML coders can link to other pages outside their own website or to pages within their own website. The Loch Ness monster site example above used an absolute URL—that means it used a full web address: http://www.lochnesssightings.com.

>> Hyperlinks use web addresses, starting with http://www., to find websites the same way the post office uses real addresses.

A local link is a link to a page on the same website the web user is already on, so it does not need the http://www to find its way there. For example: <a href="BFpics.html">Bigfoot pics</a>.

This can be difficult to practice until the coder has a website up and running on a server somewhere. It can also be done by combining any practice HTML code into a single file on a computer.

BOOKMARKS

Another great HTML linking ability is bookmarks. Bookmarks allow readers to click and jump to specific spots on a webpage. This is very useful if a webpage contains a lot of text. To link

>>HTML: JUST ONE PIECE

Climber.com, based in California, uses HTML to help top companies and high-level employees find each other in the job market. Their website gathers job and résumé information from many different sources into an online database. Then, they organize that information in a way that saves companies and job hunters many hours of work. With their Postings.com service, they take job postings from thousands of small business clients looking to hire new staff members and then automatically post the job to hundreds of job boards. In addition to HTML, Climber.com developers use MySQL, SOLR, and Ruby on Rails, a program that combines a database, a web service, and web pages. Their customers can interact with Climber.com on all devices: computer, tablet, and smartphone.

to a bookmark, the coder must first create the bookmark. For example: <h1 id="Cabra">Chubacabra Pictures</h1>.

It is possible to put a bookmark around any text, though the <h1> announces it as a header so it would be best to use it for a large or important block of text, such as the Bookmarks headline above. This will not add a hyperlink to the page; the word will not be underlined. However, it will be secretly marked in the HTML code with a bookmark, so that the browser can find it if the coder ever does want to link to it—which he or she probably does, or else the coder would not bookmark it.

When the code wants to link to that bookmark, all it needs to include is a link, such as this: <a href="#Cabra"> See Pictures of the Chubacabra </a>.

Notice the href= does not go to a website or page this time—but, instead, directly to the "#Cabra" bookmark that was just created. Now, when that link is clicked, the browser will find the id="Cabra" and bring the reader directly to it. This tool can just as easily add a link to the bookmark from another page. For example:

<a href="othercryptids.html#JD"> See Pictures of the Jersey Devil </a>

CHAPTER 4

WORTH 1,000 WORDS: ADDING IMAGES

Adding an image to a webpage is a simple procedure and opens up more options for what a designer can do with HTML. You can practice this yourself with just a few easy steps.

1. Pick an image from your computer (a .jpg, .gif, or .png are the most common web-friendly image types).

>>CREDIT WHERE IT IS DUE

Before putting any kind of image online, it is important to have permission to do so. There are copyright laws that protect most pictures. After all, a creator should get credit for his or her work anytime it is used. One way to avoid having to acquire permission is to search for and use pictures in the public domain (meaning anyone can use them). There are many websites that collect all the public domain pictures available. Also, in many cases, people are allowed "fair use" of images. This means they can

(continued on the next page)

(continued from the previous page)

use pictures for research or just to comment on for their personal website or blog—they just cannot use them to sell their own products or services. Anyone using someone else's image needs to include where he or she got the image (known as proper attribution), giving credit to the person who owns or created the image.

Bill Gates' home in Medina, Washington. (Photo: http://www.flickr.com/photos/jeffwilcox/ [CC BY 2.0], via Wikimedia Commons)

>> This picture of Bill Gates's home in Medina, Washington, gives the proper attribution and photo credit, located beneath the picture.

2. Modify the image, if needed. Maybe you want to change its size or crop it (showing only one part of the picture). There are ways for HTML to do some of this, but it is best to alter any image before you use it on a website. There are hundreds of free image editing sites online, and your computer probably has one or two also.

The best place to start is with the most basic image tag:

<img src="lochness1.jpg" alt="Loch Ness Monster">

The <img> tag is a special one-shot tag that does not require (or allow) an end tag. There is no </img>. The code above gets the job done.

The code **src=" "** provides the URL (web address) of the image. If the image file you plan to use is in the same place as your webpage—which it would be if you had a real website up somewhere—all you need is the name of the image: (lochness1. jpg). The web browser will know to look for the image in the same folder or directory as the website.

However, the image does not have to be in your website folder. It might be somewhere else on the internet. If the image file is elsewhere on the internet, you can use a complete URL. For example:

<img src="http://coolmonsters.org/pics/lochness1.jpg"
alt="Loch Ness Monster">

The web browser now knows to go to coolmonsters.org and a folder called pics to look for "lochness1.jpg." To practice, you might want to use this method to point to a picture. That way, your picture will actually appear.

The code **alt=" "** describes the image. You can put anything you want in this part. It could be a single word or a full paragraph. It is up to you. Think of it like an alternative name. If, for some reason, the real image does not load correctly, the user will now be able to at least know what the image was supposed to be.

The alternative name is mostly for visitors who cannot see your image, such as people who are visually impaired or color blind; people who have turned off images on their web browser

>>LIGHTS, MUSIC, CAMERA ... ACTION

Adding video and sound to a webpage is almost as easy as adding an image. A programmer can have sounds or a song play in the background or have the audio show up as a player that has to be clicked to start. Programmers do this by using "<audio> element":

```
<audio src="song.mp3" controls>
If you are reading this, your browser does not support the audio tag.
</audio>
```

To show a video in HTML, coders use "<video> element." For example:

```
<video width="300" height="200" controls>
<source src="movie.mp4" type="video/mp4">
If you are reading this, your browser does not support the video tag.
</video>
```

to make the program work faster; or search engines, which are constantly searching the internet for content but cannot see images and can only read alternative names.

In fact, for these good reasons, the alt= is required. A webpage will not show the page correctly without it.

SIZE AND PLACEMENT

Unless a coder tells it differently, a web browser will show the image the exact size it is in its file. Maybe that size is bigger or smaller than what the coder wants to display on the website. To change the size of an image, he or she can apply "width" and "height" attributes. For example:

```
<img src="lochness1.jpg" alt="Loch Ness Monster" width="200" height="300">
```

Programmers can also control where the image shows up on the page, whether they want it in the center or on the right, left, or bottom. They can also decide if they want the text on a page to "wrap" around their picture or to keep out of the way and let the picture stand alone. This uses CSS and can get a little trickier. This is a sample of how it works:

Aligned images do not wrap text around them. Text, instead, is placed as a block of text all by itself before or after the image.

```
<p>This is text about the Loch Ness Monster. <img src="lochness1.jpg" alt="Loch Ness Monster" width="200" height="300" style="vertical-align:bottom"/> More text about the Loch Ness Monster.</p>
```

The use of tools was first observed by Goodall when she witnessed a chimp use the stem of a branch to collect termites for food. After this groundbreaking discovery, more evidence has been found all throughout Africa. Chimpanzees use rocks as hammers; anvils to open nuts; leaves as napkins or sponges; sticks to open beehives for honey and create spears to kill small mammals.

It's a Chimp's Life

Chimps are actually great apes and not monkeys. An easy way to distinguish between the two is to look for a tail. Monkeys have tails, while apes (gorillas, orangutans, bonobos, chimpanzees, and humans) do not.

Chimpanzees are omnivores. Their diet consists mostly of fruit and leaves. However, they also tend to eat insects, bark, eggs, nuts and even smaller monkeys or other animals for meat.

Chimps are highly intelligent when it comes to foraging for food. They are capable of remembering where food is located and when a particular fruit is ripe. They will also coordinate their efforts and share the meat amongst the group. It has also been observed that some chimpanzees may consume certain plants for medicinal purposes, like soothing an upset stomach or getting rid of intestinal parasites.

Chimps are Declining

- Chimpanzees are among the most threatened primates in Africa for many reasons (Goodall 2001).
- Fifty years ago, one million chimps were living in Africa. Today, it's estimated that number has decreased to 170,000-300,000 wild chimps.

Mshindi hang from a tree branch in the Kimberly-Clark Chimpanzee Forest.

>> The text on this website is wrapped around the picture of a chimpanzee.

Floating images have text that wraps around the image, flowing around it.

```
<img src="lochness1.jpg" alt="Loch Ness Monster" width="200" height="300" style="float: left; margin: 0px 25px 25px 0px;"/>
```

LINK THIS PICTURE

Adding a hyperlink to an image makes a webpage more dynamic. Also, all those clickable menu buttons on the home page are

>>TO GIF OR NOT TO GIF, THAT IS THE QUESTION

There are three popular image formats used in web design: .jpg, .gif, and .png. Each has particular strengths and weaknesses. People want to use the format that has the best quality and smallest file size for whatever they are trying to show. Using a smaller file size helps make a webpage load faster. The .gif format is perfect for simple icons, animations, and graphics with lots of flat color, such as logos and flags. The .jpg format (unlike .gif) can display millions of colors and is fantastic for online photographs (including black and white ones). The .png format is newer and combines the .gif and .jpg formats to work well with online graphics that require transparency (a clear background), complex photographs and graphics, and images that require editing.

typically images. Adding a hyperlink to an image works almost the same as it does with text.

<a   href="   https://www.visitscotland.com"> <img   src=" lochness1.jpg" alt="Loch Ness Monster"></a>

That is all it takes. Now, clicking on the picture will take the user to www.visitscotland.com or wherever else the code tells the browser to go.

CHAPTER 5

LOOKING AT THE WHOLE

Everything discussed so far has been a specific component of using HTML on a webpage. Because HTML is so versatile, however, it can also be used to work on an entire page at once. For example:

```
<!DOCTYPE html>
<html>

<head>
   <meta charset="utf-8">
   <lang="en">
    <title>My first website!</title>
</head>

<body>
<p>This is where all my content goes.</p>
<p>And, here's some more.</p>
<p>And a random <a href="https://www.tumblr.com/"> link</a>
to enjoy.</p>
```

```
</body>

</html>
```

The first thing different about this piece of code is the <!DOCTYPE html>. This is not a tag.

The <!> is a special function that allows programmers to put in comments that people can see only if they look at the source code. These words will not appear in the browser. This is a great way for a coder to leave notes for his or her own benefit or for the benefit of someone who is looking at his or her code.

```
<!—This is hidden text. I'm working on the whole HTML page now.—>
<!—Jeff Pratt designed this site all by himself and deserves a raise!—>
```

When used as <!DOCTYPE html>, this tag lets the browser know that it is now looking at an HTML page. Yes, the browser would have figured it out eventually anyway, but it is still a nice introduction to get things ready. No excuses for the browser now—it knows exactly what it needs.

Next comes the <html> tag, which will frame the head and body text. Notice how the entire page ends with </html>, finally closing that tag. This is another way to let the browser know it is looking at a webpage written in HTML and should act accordingly.

>>BILLION DOLLAR UNICORNS BUILT IN HTML

In the business and investing world, a unicorn refers to a new tech company or online idea that is a big hit and reaches a value of $1 billion. Here are some recent unicorns built in HTML:

- Uber
- Airbnb
- Spotify
- Snapchat
- Pinterest
- Dropbox
- Snapdeal
- BuzzFeed
- CreditKarma
- Survey Monkey

>> There are countless billion-dollar ideas, including Uber and other popular apps, that are built around HTML.

Next comes the combination of the two main sections:

The <head> tells the browser specific information about the page before it is loaded for someone to look at. Most of the information in the head is only ever seen by the browser. In this example, the head covers three things.

1. <meta charset="utf-8">: This tells the browser what standard characters it should use and expect. UTF-8 the most common in the United States.

2. <lang="en">: This tells the browser what language it should use and expect.

3. <title>My first website!</title>: This tells the browser what title it should display up top when people visit the page.

The head goes above the body. That way, it can give browsers and search engines all sorts of information before the content is shown.

It is important to note that in HTML5 (the current standard), the <head> element can be omitted. The browser will figure out what to do with <lang="en">, etc., without the extra organization of putting it in "the head." Still, many sites use the <head> tag and, even if not, programmers still have to put the code that used to go in the head up at the top of the code. It is better practice to tell the browser all it needs to know before showing content.

After all that is covered, whether it is in the <head> tag or not, the body is where all the content goes.

Again, in HTML5, the <body> element is not strictly required—the browser will figure things out—but, if someone is checking website source code or working with other programmers, a programmer is still going to see the <body> </body> tags a lot as a way to organize the webpage.

CHAPTER 6

WHERE DO YOU GO FROM HERE? NEXT STEPS

W ebsites get more powerful and interactive every day, and so programmers have to improve their skills, too. After getting down the basics of HTML, beginners typically want to explore forms, CSS, and JavaScript.

FORMS

HTML has some very simple ways to collect information online and send that data back to the website to do any number of things. While this is not easy to accomplish without a dedicated server, it can still be a good tool for practicing basic HTML skills. For example, the code to create a form for submitting text might look something like this:

```
<form action="demo_only.html">
<p>First name: <input name="first" type="text">
<p>Last name: <input name="last" type="text">
<p><input type="submit">
</form>
```

The code to create a form for submitting a response from a list might look something like this:

```
<form action="demo_only.html">
<p> Which is your favorite?
<select name="monsters">
  <option value="bigfoot">Bigfoot</option>
  <option value="loch">Loch Ness Monster</option>
  <option value="chup">Chupacabra</option>
  <option value="nj">The Jersey Devil</option>
</select>
<input type="submit">
</form>
```

JAVASCRIPT

JavaScript is one of the main technologies used in most websites. It makes webpages more interactive and provides the code for many online programs, including games. This is an example of how to tie HTML and JavaScript together:

```
<html>
<body>

<button type="button" onclick="myFunction()">Click for Java!</button>

<p id="javatest">I'm learning.</p>

<script>
```

```
// ----------------------------------------

function redrawSiteWithMagic(){
    if($(window).width() < 700){
        $('.rotate-left').addClass('rota
        $('.rotate-right').addClass('rot
        $('.rotate-left').removeClass('r
        $('.rotate-right').removeClass('
    }else{
        $('.rotate-left-disactivated').a
        $('.rotate-right-disactivated').
        $('.rotate-left-disactivated').r
        $('.rotate-right-disactivated').
    }
    //---------
    if($(window).width() < 641){
        if($('nav').parent()[0].tagName

        $('body').prepend($('nav'));

        if($('nav .dropdown-toggle')
            $('nav').prepend('<a hre
```

```
m class="donate-form" method="POST" acti
<input type="hidden" name="receiver" val
<input type="hidden" name="formcomment"
<input type="hidden" name="short-dest" \
<input type="hidden" name="label" value=
<input type="hidden" name="quickpay-form
<input type="hidden" name="targets" valu
<label><input type="number" name="sumInU
<input type="hidden" name="sum" id="sum"
<!-- <input type="hidden" name="comment'
<input type="hidden" name="need-fio" val
<input type="hidden" name="need-email" v
<input type="hidden" name="need-phone" v
<input type="hidden" name="need-address"
<!-- <label><input type="radio" name="pa
<label><input type="radio" name="payment
<input type="button" id="donateBtn" valu
)rm>
    <iframe frameborder="0" allowtranspare
>
:lass="modal-footer">

>
```

INSERT MODE, Line 229, Column 9   Tab Size: 4   PHP

>> JavaScript works directly with HTML and is one of the main technologies used to make web pages more interactive.

```
function myFunction() {
    document.getElementById("javatest").innerHTML = "Hello,
World!";
}
</script>


</body>
</html>
```

If you type out this code and save it as a webpage, you should be able to click the button that says Click for Java! and see what happens. This simple program shows just some of JavaScript's capabilities. There are thousands of tricks JavaScript can do.

>>EXPANDING KNOWLEDGE

The best place to find cool JavaScript, forms, and CSS code to use is online. There are thousands of websites with examples, ideas, tutorials, and hands-on exercises to try out. Simply searching for JavaScript on a search engine will provide hundreds of ideas. Most websites will show the actual code being used. It might be difficult for a beginner to understand—learning anything new always is—but, in coding as in many other things, it is okay to make some mistakes. They are an opportunity to continue learning.

STYLE SHEETS

HTML5 really likes to use Cascading Style Sheets (CSS) to tell a web browser how it should show text and the page. Here are some examples that show how they work:

```
<html>
<head>

<style>
h1 {color: black; font-family: arial; font-size: 200%;}
p  {color: red; font-family: times; font-size: 120%; }
</style>

</head>
```

```
<body>
<h1>This is text in a heading</h1>
<p>This is text in a paragraph.</p>
</body>

</html>
```

There are two things to notice in this code: The <style> goes in the "head" of the HTML document so the browser sees it before the text it is supposed to show; and all the info being shared between the { } symbols tells the browser that every time it sees <h1> later, that text should be shown in black, in Arial font, and 200% the default size.

Coders can also control the way web browsers show links using styles. By default, a link will appear in specific colors:

An unvisited link is underlined and blue.

A visited link is underlined and purple.

An active link is underlined and red.

It is possible to change the default colors, for example, like so:

```
<style>
a:link {color: green; background-color: transparent; text-decoration: none;}
a:visited {color: pink; background-color: transparent; text-decoration: none;}
a:hover {color: red; background-color: transparent; text-decoration: underline;}
a:active {color: yellow; background-color: transparent; text-decoration: underline;}
</style>
```

>>GETTING STARTED

Bill Gates—cofounder of Microsoft and one of the richest people in the world—first started coding in middle school when the Mothers' Club at his school used some money from a recent garage sale to buy a computer for the students. During lunch,

(continued on the next page)

>> Shown here, a young Bill Gates, now one of the richest people on Earth, is just getting started, dreaming of how his programming skills might help shape the future.

(continued from the previous page)

Gates would work on his code, and he soon wrote his first computer program: a computerized game of tic-tac-toe. By the time he was sixteen, Gates and a school friend started their first company: they wrote a program to read and show data of traffic reports.

Mark Zuckerberg—cofounder of Facebook and also one of the richest people in the world—first started coding when he was ten, and his dad—who was a computer hobbyist—invited his son to try out the new office computer. His father was a dentist and, together, the two wrote a program titled ZuckNet, which connected their home computer with the computer in the office to alert "Doctor Z" when a patient arrived. Mark read books on coding, started studying with a coding tutor, and took a college class in computer science while still in middle school. In college, he majored in computer science. Thanks to Facebook, Zuckerberg was a millionaire by the time he was twenty-two and a billionaire by twenty-three.

You should be able to type the above code into your HTML file and test it out with some hyperlinks. The style code needs to go in the head above all the links, but only has to be typed once.

After experimenting with the exercises and examples in this book, there are many places to go to learn more.

The first option will be, of course, the internet. There are thousands of online tutorials and online communities built to help you learn web development. Most of them are free. The internet was built on the sharing of information and code. Computer programmers like to help new programmers.

There are also thousands of books. You will find a recommended list in this book to get you started. You can borrow programming books at your own school or local library or buy some from your favorite bookstore. Find out if your school offers any computer programming classes. Or see if there is a club or organization in your community that provides coding classes. Many do—you just have to look.

At some point, you will want to have your own website or blog to really test out some code. This will let you do more things with images and forms and will help you get a feel for how a website works. There are many places to find a website you can customize with your own code. Most blog sites—and many websites—are free.

Remember not to share personal information online—this includes your address, phone number, little brother's name, or anything else you would not want a stranger to know. The internet is a wonderful thing—it helps the world to share unlimited information. Unfortunately, there are also some bad folks out there, and you should always keep yourself safe.

In college, you can take classes in computer science and software development. You could also work in internships and take courses that teach specific coding languages, too.

HTML and CSS are a great start, but they are only the first steps to a career in web development. Next, you will want to take on harder (and more powerful) coding languages, such as JavaScript, Jquery, and then—to work more with databases— PHP, MySQL, and then Python and Ruby. You will learn more as you go along and be ready for the next language after you have mastered the last. It all ties back to HTML, so you are off to a great start.

GLOSSARY

BLOG A regularly updated website or webpage, typically run by an individual or small group, often written in an informal style.

BOOKMARK A special link that provides a shortcut to a specific spot on another page or somewhere on the same page.

COLLABORATIVE AUTHORING Written work created by multiple people working together (collaboratively) at the same time.

CSS Cascading Style Sheets is a special language used to describe the presentation of a document written in a markup language like HTML.

DATABASE A computer specifically designed to gather and organize information and data.

FAIR USE The legal term (in US copyright law) that provides for some usage of copyright material (images or text) without the need for permission from, or payment to, the copyright holder.

FONT A set of characters used in text in one style or size.

HTML Hypertext Markup Language is the standardized system for showing text files and websites on the web.

HYPERLINK A link to another computer location or file, activated by clicking on a highlighted word or image.

INTERNET A global network that allows computers worldwide to connect and exchange information.

JAVASCRIPT A computer programming language used to create interactive effects within web browsers.

NESTING A common programming technique in which the code is listed in a particular organized order.

SOCIAL MEDIA A collection of websites and applications

designed to allow people to share content quickly and easily. Some examples of social media platforms are Twitter, Instagram, and Snapchat.

SOURCE CODE The computer instructions or code written out, usually as plain text.

TAG HTML tags are keywords in the code that are hidden from the user but define how your web browser should display the content.

UNICORN A new company in the software or technology industry already valued at more than a billion dollars.

WEB BROWSERS Software that retrieves and presents information on the web. Some examples of web browsers are Microsoft Internet Explorer, Apple Safari, Mozilla Firefox, and Google Chrome.

WEB CRAWLER A program that continually searches and then catalogs the entire web in a systematic way, looking for new data and pages.

W3C The main international organization for the development of standards for the World Wide Web.

HTML Writers Guild
556 S. Fair Oaks Avenue, #101-200
Pasadena, CA 91105
Website: http://hwg.org
The organization is the first and largest international association for website design. Membership is open to anyone with an interest in learning more about website design and development.

International Web Association (IWA)
556 S. Fair Oaks Avenue, #101-200
Pasadena, CA 91105
(626) 449-3709
Website: http://iwanet.org
IWA provides educational and certification standards for web professionals and has more than 300,000 members in 106 countries. IWA provides web certification and education programs, specialized employment resources, and technical assistance to individuals and businesses.

Internet Society (ISOC)
1775 Wiehle Avenue
Reston, VA 20190
(703) 439-2120
Website: https://www.internetsociety.org
Facebook: @InternetSociety
Twitter: @internetsociety
Instagram: @internetsociety/
YouTube: @InternetSocietyVideo

This global and diverse cause-driven organization is dedicated
to ensuring that the internet stays open, transparent, and is
defined by the users.

Webgrrls International
119 W 72nd Street, #314
New York, NY 10023
(888) 932-4775
Website: http://webgrrls.com
Facebook and Twitter: @Webgrrls
Webgrrls' mission is to empower women through technology
and encourage them to learn to use technology and the
tools of the internet to help them propel their careers and
reach their goals.

World Organization of Webmasters
PO Box 584
Washington, IL 61571-0584
(662) 493-2776
Email: membership@webprofessionals.org
Website: https://webprofessionals.org
Facebook: @webprofessionals
Twitter: @webprominute
YouTube: @WebProfessionals/videos
This nonprofit professional association is dedicated to the
support of individuals and organizations who create,
manage, or market websites. It also provides education and
training resources as well as certification for aspiring
programmers.

World Wide Web Consortium (W3C)

W3C/MIT

32 Vassar Street

Room 32-386

Cambridge, MA 02139

(617) 253-2613

Website: https://www.w3.org

Twitter: @W3C

W3C is the main international organization for the development of standards for the World Wide Web. W3C also supports education, develops software, and provides an open forum for discussion about the web.

World Wide Web Foundation

1110 Vermont Avenue NW, Suite 500

Washington, DC 20005

(202) 595-2892

Website: https://webfoundation.org

Facebook and Twitter: @webfoundation

The Web Foundation, as it is known, promotes "digital equality" across the world so that everyone has the right to access the internet freely and fully. It works with governments and businesses to unlock the benefits of the web for everyone equally.

FOR FURTHER READING

Bedell, J. M. *So, You Want to Be a Coder? The Ultimate Guide to a Career in Programming, Video Game Creation, Robotics, and More!* New York, NY: Aladdin, 2016.

Birly, Shane. *How to Be a Blogger and Vlogger in 10 Easy Lessons.* Lake Forest, CA: Walter Foster Jr., 2016.

Connor, Joseph. *Programming: Computer Programming for Beginners: Learn the Basics of HTML5, JavaScript & CSS.* Newcastle Upon Tyne, UK: MJG Publishing, 2017.

Freedman, Jeri. *Careers in Computer Science and Programming.* New York, NY: Rosen Publishing, 2011.

Harmon, Daniel E. *Powering Up a Career in Software Development and Programming.* New York, NY: Rosen Publishing, 2016.

Harris, Andrew. *HTML5 and CSS3 All-in-One For Dummies.* 3rd ed. Hoboken, NJ: John Wiley & Sons, 2014.

Harris, Patricia. *What Is HTML Code?* New York, NY: PowerKids Press, 2018.

Martin, Chris. *Build Your Own Web Site.* New York, NY: Rosen Publishing, 2014.

Minnick, Chris. *JavaScript For Kids.* Hoboken, NJ: John Wiley & Sons, 2015.

Niver, Heather Moore. *Careers for Tech Girls in Computer Science.* New York, NY: Rosen Publishing, 2016.

Poolos, Jamie. *Designing, Building, and Maintaining Websites.* New York, NY: Rosen Publishing, 2017.

Young Rewired State. *Get Coding! Learn HTML, CSS & JavaScript & Build a Website, App & Game.* Somerville, MA: Candlewick, 2017.

BIBLIOGRAPHY

Becraft, Michael. *Bill Gates: A Biography*. Santa Barbara, CA: Greenwood, 2014.

Blum, Andrew. *Tubes: A Journey to the Center of the Internet*. New York, NY: Ecco, 2013.

CBInsights. "The Global Unicorn Club." https://www. cbinsights.com/research-unicorn-companies. Retrieved February 12, 2018.

Dodd, Christopher. *How I Learned to Code: Lessons from Teaching Myself Web Development and Becoming a Paid Programmer in Only 3 Months*. CreateSpace, 2016.

Duckett, Jon. *Web Design with HTML, CSS, JavaScript and JQuery Set*. Hoboken, NJ: John Wiley & Sons, Inc., 2014.

Hafner, Katie. *Where Wizards Stay Up Late: The Origins of the Internet*. New York, NY: Simon & Schuster, 1996.

Kroll, Luisa, and Kerry Dolan (eds). "Meet the Members of the Three-Comma Club." *Forbes, March 6, 2018*. https://www .forbes.com/billionaires. https://www.html5rocks.com.

Mezric, Ben. *The Accidental Billionaires*. New York, NY: Anchor, 2010.

w3schools.com. "HTML5 Tutorial." https://www.w3schools. com/html. Retrieved February 12, 2018. https://www .w3.org.

INDEX

ABOUT THE AUTHOR

Jeff Pratt first started coding for fun in 1983 on a Commodore 64 in a computer language called PET BASIC. Twelve years later, he taught himself a brand-new computer language called HTML. Since then, he's worked as a webmaster, software developer, and senior consultant for e-business for companies across the country. He has taught HTML and web design through one-on-one training and in group seminars and was the radio host of the weekly program *MY COMPUTER*. He earned certification in software development from the University of Cincinnati in 2000. He lives in Ohio with two dogs and a lizard named Zeus.

PHOTO CREDITS

Cover oliveromg/Shutterstock.com; cover, back cover, pp. 1, 4–5 (background) © iStockphoto.com/letoakin; p. 5 Rose Carson /Shutterstock.com; pp. 6, 36, 40 Rosen Publishing; p. 8 FPG /Archive Photos/Getty Images; p. 9 Rick Friedman/Corbis News /Getty Images; p. 11 Eric Vandeville/Gamma-Rapho/Getty Images; p. 12 Zurijeta/Shutterstock.com; p. 14 Best-Backgrounds /Shutterstock.com; p. 17 tom_tom_13/Shutterstock.com; p. 19 Gil C/Shutterstock.com; p. 21 dennizn/Shutterstock.com; p. 28 Frank Gaertner/Shutterstock.com; p. 29 Artseen/Shutterstock .com; p. 32 Jakub Krechowicz/Shutterstock.com; p. 44 TY Lim /Shutterstock.com; p. 48 An147yus/Shutterstock.com; p. 51 Deborah Feingold/Corbis Historical/Getty Images.

Design and Layout: Nicole Russo-Duca; Editor: Siyavush Saidian; Photo Researcher: Nicole DiMella